MW00809714

OUTDOOR
— SKILLS —
HANDBOOK

CAMPFIRE COOKING

Bear Grylls

This survival skills handbook has been specially put together to help young explorers like you to stay safe in the wild. When you're spending a night in the wild, a nutritious, hot meal is a real treat, especially after a long day, but cooking outdoors can be a bit of a challenge! This book will teach you how to start a fire and rustle up some tasty treats using a campfire or camping stove. Remember: a good cook in the wild is always a popular teammate!

Bear.

CONTENTS

Bear Grylls

CAMPFIRES AND COOKING

Making fire is an ancient skill that humans have practiced over hundreds of thousands of years. Its discovery first set our ancestors on the path to civilization. The ability to make fire is still a vital survival skill, especially for explorers.

Invention of fire

Tens of thousands of years ago, early humans learned to make fire by striking flints or rubbing sticks together. Nowadays, we mostly use matches or lighters, but it's still handy to learn the traditional techniques, too (see pages 10–13).

Why do we need fire?

Fire is incredibly helpful. Here are just some of its many uses:

- Produces light, which is especially useful at night.
- Produces heat to warm our bodies and dry wet clothes.
- For preparing food and hot drinks.
- For purifying water.
- Provides protection against dangerous animals and biting insects.
- Provides a place to gather with friends, which boosts group morale.
- For signaling for help in an emergency.
- It is nature's TV! Everyone likes to watch it!

Campfire cooking

Nothing beats the taste of a meal prepared outdoors on a campfire, camping stove, or grill! A hot meal is delicious after a long day's hike, and cooking your own food outdoors can be a lot of fun! Turn to pages 20–45 to find some recipes for nourishing and tasty campfire meals.

Safety warning

Fire making and campfire cooking are great fun, but can also be dangerous. Be very careful around fires, and never leave a fire unattended. Always have a bucket of water or a fire blanket handy so you can put out a fire if necessary. Hot cooking pots can burn you, so always use oven mitts or tongs. Beware of hot steam, which can be just as dangerous as boiling water.

BEAR SAYS

Some campsites forbid lighting fires, but you may be allowed to use a barbecue grill or a camping stove. Always obey the campsite rules and be aware of the dangers of forest fires.

look out for signs telling you if fires are allowed or not

PREPARING YOUR FIRE

The key to a good fire is thorough preparation. Gather all the materials you need and stack them within reach before you begin. This will save you a lot of time and energy once you start.

Fire pyramid

A successful fire depends on three things: heat, fuel, and oxygen. (Just like humans!) Remove any one of these, and the fire will go out. Vary the three factors to control your fire. For example, fan a fire to increase oxygen and make it bigger, or smother it to starve it of oxygen and make it smaller or put it out. Adding more fuel will also make your fire bigger and last longer.

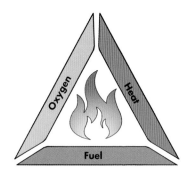

Gathering materials

Assemble all the materials you need: tinder will take the spark and kindling will feed the flames. You will then need wood of different thicknesses to fuel the fire.

- **Tinder** Dry grass, straw, birch bark, sawdust, pine needles, animal fur, tissue paper, and scrunched-up newspaper all make good tinder when bone dry.
- **Kindling** Dry twigs about 3/4 inch across make good kindling. You can also use wood shavings, or split dry softwood with an axe.
- **Fuel** Feed the fire with small logs or split wood, then larger logs.

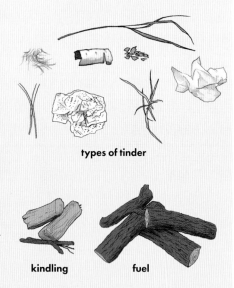

types of tinder

kindling   fuel

Choose your location

Build your fire on level ground, away from trees or overhanging branches. Site it well away from tents, and downwind of your campsite, otherwise you risk drifting sparks igniting the fabric. Clear the ground of sticks and moss that could cause the fire to spread.

BEAR SAYS

Don't use wet or damp wood on a campfire—it's hard to light and will make the fire smoky. You can dry damp tinder in your pockets and store it in a plastic bag.

Building a fire reflector

A fire reflector acts as a windshield and directs the heat for warmth and cooking.

1. Build your fire reflector upwind of your fire.
2. Hammer two stout stakes into the ground about 12 inches apart.
3. Hammer another pair about 3 feet away, parallel to the first two.
4. Place long sticks between the upright stakes to form a screen.

FIRE STRUCTURES

You can build a campfire using several different structures, depending on conditions and how you want to use the fire. For example, a slow-burning, steady fire provides background warmth, while a hot fire is best for cooking.

Tepee

This simple, cone-shaped fire is quite easy to build and light. You can make a tepee fire by leaning several small sticks together above a ball of kindling to make a pyramid, or tepee, shape. This is the most basic shape for fire lighting, and the fire can be fed with bigger logs as it burns.

BEAR SAYS

Place damp kindling and fuel by the campfire to dry it out, but be careful not to set it alight!

Pyramid

A pyramid, or temple, fire uses a lot of wood but will burn for hours. Lay two large logs at the base around a small tepee fire. Place four slightly smaller logs on top, then smaller logs on top of that to form a pyramid. Light it from the side. As the fire burns down, the topmost logs will fall in to fuel the blaze.

Fire pit with stones

A fire pit is very handy. It will protect a fire in windy conditions, and stop it from spreading and damaging the surrounding area. Dig a shallow pit and build a tepee fire in it. Surround the fire with a ring of stones to contain it and reflect heat.

Star shape

Build a tepee fire and position four large logs in a cross with their ends in the fire. Push them further in as they burn down. This structure is good if you only have large logs for fuel.

Trapper fire

Build a tepee fire between two large, green (newly cut and sap-filled) logs. These will contain the fire, preventing it from spreading, and protecting the flames from wind.

Fire platform

Lay a platform of small, green sticks underneath your campfire to protect the fire from wet ground or snow.

FIRE LIGHTING

Now that you've built your fire, your next task is to light it! The easiest way to do this is by using a lighter or matches, but if you don't have either on hand there are plenty of other techniques you can try.

How to light a campfire

1. Build a small tepee fire with a ball of tinder in the center. Leave gaps so that air can reach the tinder. Strike a match or put a lighter to the tinder.
2. Blow gently to fan the ember. After the tinder has caught fire, add small and then larger sticks to feed the flames.

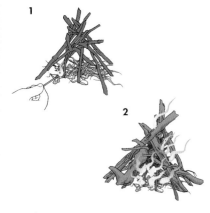

Using matches

Strike a match, always in the direction away from your body. Cup your hand around the flame to shield it from wind. Tilt the match head down so that it burns a little before you put it to the tinder.

Firesteel

This is a steel rod attached to a thin strip of metal called a "striker." Place the tip of the rod in the tinder and brace the striker against it. Then push the scraper down to direct hot sparks onto the tinder.

Magnifying glass

A magnifying glass will ignite dry tinder in strong sunlight. Hold the glass at an angle to direct a beam of light onto the tinder. Be patient, and eventually it will start to smoke. Blow very gently to ignite a flame.

BEAR SAYS

Fire lighting can be very dangerous if you aren't careful. Never start a fire without a responsible adult nearby.

Fire starters

Fire starters are small, solid fuel packets, often soaked in flammable liquid, that you can buy in many stores. They're very useful if other techniques fail, or in windy conditions. Break the block into small pieces and place a few bits in the tinder. Wash your hands after handling fire starters.

How to make a fuzz stick

This is a partially shaved piece of wood that can be used to start a fire if tinder is in short supply. You will need a dry stick, thicker than your finger. Run your pocketknife down the wood to create long shavings. Stop before you reach the end so that you don't detach the shavings. Always cut away from your body. Repeat this until you have several rings of shavings running up the stick.

ADVANCED FIRE CRAFT

To be a true survival expert, you need to learn how to light a fire without matches or a lighter. There are several different methods. All require friction, or rubbing, to ignite the tinder. It takes a lot of patience, but it's a great skill to master!

Fire plow

You need: hardwood stick, softwood base board, pocketknife or chisel

1. Cut a long, straight groove in the base board using a pocketknife or chisel.
2. Make a point on one end of the hardwood stick.
3. Pressing hard, repeatedly push the pointed end up and down in the groove. The friction will produce heat, and eventually a small ember. This ember can be added to your dry tinder, which, when gently fanned, will ignite.

Hand drill

You need: straight stick, base board, pocketknife

1. Smooth the sides of a long, straight stick, and round one end. Hold the rounded end on the base board near the side and draw around it. Carve a shallow, stick-sized hollow in the base board, then a notch at the edge. Place an ember pan or leaf under the notch to catch an ember.
2. Hold the board steady with your foot or knee, as shown. Place the stick in the hollow and roll it quickly between your palms, running your hands down the stick as you roll. Hot ember dust will fall into the notch which can be collected, tipped into your tinder, and fanned into a flame.

Flames from an ember

Once you have an ember, add it to your dry tinder, such as straw or scrunched-up paper, and fan or wave it gently back and forth through the air, until it ignites. Be gentle and don't blow too hard, or you will blow it out!

Overnight fire

To keep a campfire lit overnight, place large logs on it and cover it lightly with earth or ashes. Don't use dry leaf mold, which will make the fire flare up again.

Extinguish a fire

Allow the fire to burn all the way down, then sprinkle water over the embers or smother them with earth to make sure the fire is fully out.

BEAR SAYS

Make sure a fire is completely out before leaving the campsite. When the ash is cold, remove any debris and sweep earth over the site.

CAMPFIRE KITCHEN

To cook outdoors, you will need pots and pans and some basic kitchen equipment. On sites where you're not allowed to have a campfire, you can usually use a grill or portable stove.

Stoves

Stoves are easy to light, and provide instant heat that you can control. Different designs burn gas, kerosene, or solid fuel. Most are light to carry or come in a handy case. Always test the stove before your trip to make sure it is in working order, and be sure to bring enough fuel!

BEAR SAYS

Never light a stove inside a tent. This is a major fire hazard! Position your stove away from tents as you would a campfire.

windshield stove

push-button stove

Barbecue grills

Barbecue grills may use charcoal, which burns hotter than wood. This makes them a good option for food that needs cooking well, such as meat. There are many designs. You can buy a disposable grill or even build your own using bricks and a grill pan.

double burner stove

portable grills

Cooking kit

A light "nest" of pans can be used on a stove, while heavy-duty pots or pans are needed to cook on an open fire. Don't bring your family's best cooking pans, as fire will blacken the outsides.

camping teakettle

portable stove and light pans

portable dishware set

cooking over a campfire using a heavy pan

camping utensil sets

portable dishwashing set

Ice chests

An ice chest keeps food, such as dairy products, fresh. Freezer blocks work like ice and can be refrozen at some campsites. If you don't have an ice chest, you can wrap a damp towel around items such as milk to keep them cold. You can also cool bottles in a stream, but be careful they don't get washed away!

CAMPFIRE STORES

Your campfire kitchen should contain some basic items, plus any specific ingredients you need for each meal. Plan detailed menus in advance so that you have everything you need. Don't wait until you've started cooking to discover you've left a vital ingredient behind!

Basic stores
These basic foods will be needed for many dishes.

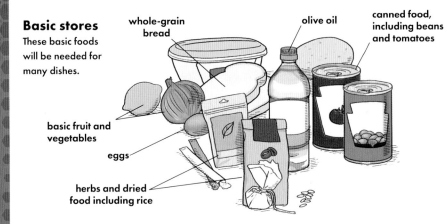

whole-grain bread

olive oil

canned food, including beans and tomatoes

basic fruit and vegetables

eggs

herbs and dried food including rice

Seasoning
Ingredients such as salt, pepper, and dried herbs provide flavor. You can also use stock cubes, curry spices, mustard, chili flakes, ketchup, or chutney to season your food.

Dried and canned foods
Dried foods are light to carry. Canned foods are heavy but keep for a long time. Canned foods such as lentils, beans, and chickpeas are precooked, so are easy to use.

Wild foods

Foods found in the wild can be added to your stores. Wild garlic, oregano, mint, and basil all add flavor to food. Wild arugula is great in salads. Fruit and berries, such as apples, plums, and raspberries, can be gathered in season, as can edible fungi, like field mushrooms. Nuts, such as sweet chestnuts, can be cooked on the campfire. Be careful—you need to be absolutely sure you have identified plants, fruits, and fungi correctly, as some are highly poisonous. Do not eat anything you have found in the wild unless an adult with knowledge of plant identification says it's safe. If in doubt, especially with mushrooms, leave them out!

Balanced diet

A healthy diet should contain a wide variety of foods, including protein and carbohydrates. Fresh fruit and vegetables provide vitamins, minerals, and also fiber, which is good for digestion. A balanced diet also contains some fat and sugar, and a little salt.

limited fat
and sugar

dairy

meat, eggs,
and fish

vegetables

fruit

whole grains

COOKING METHODS

There are as many methods of cooking outdoors—using a campfire, barbecue grill, or stove—as there are indoors in a kitchen. Food can be grilled, roasted, fried, boiled, or baked, plus there are some new and exciting outdoor techniques you can try.

Building a tripod

A tripod provides a sturdy support for a teakettle or cooking pot. You will need three long, straight sticks. Bind one end of the sticks together with a cord, and fan out the other ends and adjust them to form a stable, three-legged structure. Hang a hook from the cord, then hang a pot or teakettle from the hook.

Making a pot holder

First, cut several notches in both ends of a long, straight stick. Then push a short, forked stick into the ground. Rest the long stick in the fork and anchor the other end to the ground firmly, using string and a tent peg. Use more string to hang a pot over your fire, using the notches on the raised end.

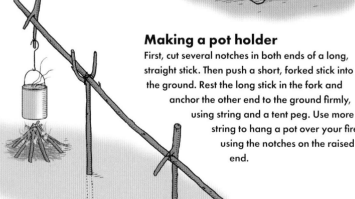

Using a barbecue grill

Light a barbecue grill 40–50 minutes before you plan to use it. This allows the flames to die down and create a bed of glowing, red-hot charcoal on which to cook.

Spit roasting

Meat, fish, and other foods can be roasted on a spit suspended over a campfire. Use green wood to make the spit, as it is less flammable and won't catch fire. Turn the spit regularly to make sure the food is cooked thoroughly and evenly.

Baking in foil

Fish, meat, potatoes, and fruit all taste great baked in foil in the embers of a campfire. Thick foil is best since it won't tear. Wrap the foil around your food to form an airtight package. Use tongs to place it in, and later to remove it from the fire to protect your hands. Cooking time depends on the food and size of the package. Carefully open one end of the package to check if the food is cooked. Beware of hot steam and fat escaping.

BEAR SAYS

Whatever method you use, make sure the food is cooked all the way through. You don't want to get food poisoning in the wild!

TIME FOR BREAKFAST

Exploring the wild can be hard work, so it's important to start your day with a healthy, nourishing breakfast to give you lots of energy for the day ahead.

Oatmeal

oats
($^1/_2$ cup per person)

milk or milk substitute
($^1/_2$ cup per person)

cinnamon

maple syrup or honey

banana (sliced)

Method

1. Put the oats in a pan. Add the milk slowly, stirring with a wooden spoon. Sprinkle on the cinnamon. Bring to a boil on medium heat.
2. Continue to cook on low heat for about five minutes until all the liquid is absorbed, and the mixture is thick and creamy. Add a little water if the oatmeal is too thick.
3. Serve in a bowl with the sliced banana. Drizzle with maple syrup or honey.

1

2

3

Scottish oatmeal

This traditional Scottish breakfast is salty, not sweet. This version uses water instead of milk. Cook in the same way, but sprinkle a little salt on top instead of syrup or sugar.

Granola, fruit, and yogurt

granola

yogurt

your favorite fruit

honey

Method

1. You can use any fruit you like for this, but berries, melon, grapes, and banana work especially well. Chop the fruit and place it in a bowl.
2. Add granola and a big dollop of Greek yogurt and some honey.

START WITH AN EGG

Eggs are packed with protein, which gives you energy. This makes them a great breakfast food to start the day with when you are out camping.

Scrambled eggs

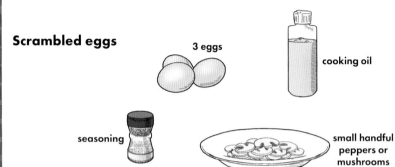

3 eggs

cooking oil

seasoning

small handful peppers or mushrooms

Method

1. Break the eggs into a bowl. Add a pinch of seasoning and then beat the mixture with a fork. You can also add a splash of milk to make your eggs extra fluffy.
2. Heat a tablespoon of oil in a pan and place over medium heat. Add the peppers or mushrooms and cook through. Stir in the eggs with a wooden spoon to prevent the mixture from sticking as it cooks.
3. Serve hot.

1

2

3

Options:

Scrambled eggs go well with smoked salmon on some whole-grain toast for a real treat.

Egg bread (French toast)

one egg
per person

cooking oil

seasoning

sliced bread

BEAR SAYS

Remove eggs from the heat just before all the egg is set, as the mixture will continue cooking in the hot pan.

Method

1. Break the egg into a shallow dish and add seasoning. Whisk with a fork until smooth. You can also add a splash of milk to make your eggs extra fluffy.
2. Dip one side of the bread in the egg mixture until thoroughly coated. Flip over and coat the other side.
3. Fry a little oil in a frying pan over medium heat. When the oil starts to sizzle, place the bread in the pan. Cook for about two minutes until golden. Flip the bread over and cook the other side. Serve hot.

1

2

3

SPEEDY LUNCHES

These tasty dishes can be whipped up on a stove or campfire for a lunchtime treat that will keep you going for the rest of the day.

Spanish omelet

4 eggs

cooked potatoes

cooking oil

1/2 onion

tomato

red or green pepper

can of corn (optional)

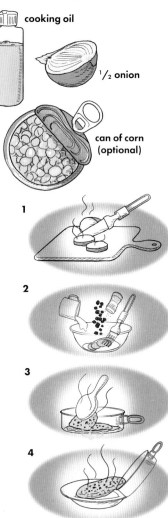

1

2

3

4

Method

1. Slice the cooked potatoes. Finely chop the onion, pepper, and tomato. Melt a little cooking oil in a frying pan over medium heat. Fry the onions until golden, stirring with a spoon.

2. Meanwhile, break the eggs into a bowl, add a little milk and salt and pepper, and whisk with a fork. Add the chopped pepper, potatoes, and tomatoes.

3. Pour the egg mixture into the pan. Use a wooden spoon to make pockets in the cooked egg to allow the remaining runny egg to cook.

4. Slide a spatula underneath and flip the omelet over to cook the other side. When cooked, slide onto a plate. Cut into wedges and serve hot or cold.

Toasted bruschetta

olive oil

seasoning

whole-grain bread

tomatoes

olives

red onion

1

2
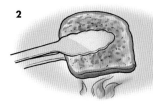

Method

1. Chop the tomatoes, onion, and olives into cubes and mix them together in a bowl. Drizzle them with olive oil and add salt and pepper if you like.
2. Toast the bread over a fire or grill, turning after two minutes, until both sides are browned.
3. Top each slice of toast with a big dollop of the tomato mixture. Eat right away.

3

CHICKEN CASSEROLE AND MASHED POTATOES

This hearty main meal is quick to assemble, but needs to be cooked slowly on a stove or campfire. Serve with mashed potatoes.

Chicken casserole

chicken breasts cut into chunks

seasoning

canned tomatoes

onion

garlic

zucchini

leek

mushrooms

red pepper

cooking oil

Method
Cooking time: About 1 hour

1. Chop the onion and vegetables and finely chop the garlic. Heat two tablespoons of oil in a large saucepan. Fry the onions, garlic, and seasoning over medium heat.
2. When the onions start to brown, add the chicken and cook for five minutes, stirring with a spoon to make sure the meat is cooked through.
3. Now add the chopped vegetables and canned tomatoes and mix well. When the mixture comes to a boil, turn it down. Put the lid on and cook over low heat for about 60 minutes, stirring occasionally. Add a little water if the casserole gets too dry.

1

2

3

Mashed potatoes

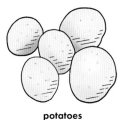

potatoes

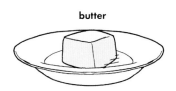

butter

milk

Method

1. Peel the potatoes and add them to a saucepan of cold water.
2. Bring to a boil and cook over medium heat for about 20 minutes until the potatoes are cooked through. Remove from the heat and drain the water.
3. Add the butter, a dash of milk, and seasoning, and mash with a potato masher or a fork.

1

2

3

BEAR SAYS

Potatoes are very easy to cook over a campfire or on a stove, but are very heavy to carry, so might not be the best food if you need to carry your food a long way.

VEGGIE STEW

This tasty and nutritious meal can be made with almost any vegetables, including ones you've foraged from the wild. Along with being warming, it's a great source of vitamins and nutrients to keep you healthy and happy on your adventures.

You will need:

sweet potatoes

garlic

zucchini

olive oil

onion

carrots

vegetable stock
(1 cup)

rosemary

seasoning

lemon

BEAR SAYS

If you are foraging your own vegetables, only eat something if an experienced adult tells you it's OK to eat. If in doubt, don't eat it!

1

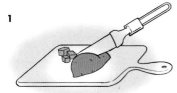

2

3

4

5

Method

1. Chop the onion, garlic, and vegetables.
2. Heat a little oil in a large pan, then add the garlic and onion. Fry for around three minutes.
3. Add a cup of vegetable stock and cook for another three minutes, allowing it to simmer gently.
4. Add the chopped sweet potatoes, zucchini, carrots, and any other vegetable you would like. Add salt and pepper to taste. Cook for 30 minutes over the campfire.
5. Squeeze in some lemon juice, give it a stir, and cook for another 30 minutes or until the vegetables are nice and golden. Serve hot.

Tip: this recipe is delicious by itself, or with chopped chicken breast, chunks of sausage, or meat substitute. Make sure you cook any meat all the way through.

CHILI CON CARNE

Add some spice to an evening around the campfire with this simple but tasty dish. It's traditionally cooked with ground beef, but tastes just as good with meat substitute, or just beans and vegetables. Add more chili to make it extra fiery!

You need:

ground beef or meat substitute ($^3/_4$ pound)

onion

garlic

fresh chili or chili powder

canned kidney beans

canned chopped tomatoes

quick-cooking rice

cooking oil

mixed herbs

plain Greek yog

BEAR SAYS

Chilies can be very hot, so use with caution! You can use three tablespoons of sweet chili sauce instead of fresh chilies or chili powder.

Method

1. Chop the onion and any extra vegetables (if using), and finely chop the garlic. Heat a little oil in a pan.
2. Fry the onions and garlic over medium heat for about 10 minutes until golden. Add the herbs, seasoning, and chili powder or chilies, and cook for a few minutes.
3. Add the beef and cook for about seven minutes while stirring to brown the meat.
4. Add the chopped vegetables, canned tomatoes, and meat substitute if you are using it instead of beef. Bring to a boil, then turn down and simmer over low heat for about 45 minutes. Add the beans near the end of the cooking time.
5. Serve over rice and add a dollop of Greek yogurt to cool it down if it's too spicy.

Quick basmati rice

1. Measure half a cup of rice per person. You will need double that amount of water. Bring the water to a boil in a pan, then add the rice. Stir once and put the lid on.
2. Cook for 10 minutes or according to the instructions on the package. Sample with a fork to check if it is cooked, then drain away any remaining water.

BAKED POTATO MEDLEY

Baked potatoes are a campsite staple! They're warm, filling, and easy to cook. Add a bit of variety to them by preparing a range of different fillings, and serve with butter.

You need:

medium-sized potatoes

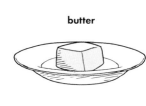

butter

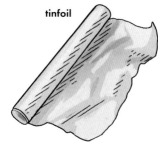

tinfoil

Method

1. Prick the potatoes with a fork. Smear the skins with butter and double-wrap in tinfoil. Use tongs to bury the potato in the hot ashes or coals of a campfire or barbecue grill.

2. Cook for 30 minutes to an hour. Use tongs to turn the potatoes occasionally. Remove one potato and poke it with a fork to see if it's cooked. When cooked, remove foil, split with a knife, and add the filling. Serve with a tablespoon of butter and a pinch of salt and pepper.

1

2

Fillings

The great thing about baked potatoes is that they offer so much variety, with an endless list of tasty fillings you can add!

Red pepper and hummus

You need: red pepper, homemade or packaged hummus

Chop the red pepper into cubes, removing the seeds and white pith. Top your potato with a good dollop of hummus, and sprinkle with red pepper.

Beans and salsa

You need: can of black or kidney beans, homemade or packaged salsa

Drain the can of beans. Mix the beans into the salsa, and spoon onto your potato. This is delicious with a squeeze of lemon juice.

Goat cheese and chives

You need: goat cheese, chopped chives

Slice the goat cheese and add to your potato. If the cheese is particularly soft, just add a spoonful or two. Top with a sprinkling of chopped chives.

Different flavors

Baked potatoes also taste delicious with guacamole, mushrooms, and sour cream. This is your chance to experiment with all sorts of different flavors and ingredients. Why not try using the chili from pages 30–31? For a tasty, healthy alternative, try baking sweet potatoes instead.

BEAR SAYS

Baked potatoes take a long time to cook, so start cooking well before you want to eat. Hot ashes are very dangerous, so ask an adult to use the tongs.

GRILLED CHICKEN AND VEGETABLES

This tasty dish can be cooked in a tinfoil package in the hot embers of a campfire, or in the coals of a barbecue grill. You can cook almost any combination of chopped meat and vegetables in this way.

You need:

chicken breast

red pepper

zucchini

broccoli

onion

chili pepper

garlic

BEAR SAYS

Be very careful when cooking with chicken. It should be kept chilled and will not stay fresh for long.

Method

1. Cook the chicken over an open fire, or on a barbecue grill, making sure both sides are browned and the meat is thoroughly cooked in the middle.
2. Chop the vegetables into chunks. Then finely dice the chili pepper and garlic.
3. Wrap the vegetables in tinfoil, adding the chopped chilies and garlic for flavor.
4. Place in the embers of your campfire using tongs. Cook for 20 minutes, then remove the foil package from the fire carefully, again using tongs. Add the vegetables to your grilled chicken and eat hot, being careful of hot juices.

1

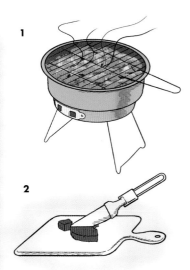

2

3

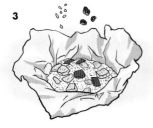

4

✗ BEAR SAYS

If you don't want chicken, why not try making this recipe with fresh fish instead?

MUSHROOM AND GOAT CHEESE BURGERS

Burgers don't have to be unhealthy—you can cook up some delicious, healthy burgers on a campfire with just a few ingredients.

You need:

olive oil

balsamic vinegar

whole-grain burger buns

garlic

seasoning

red pepper

portobello mushrooms

arugula

goat cheese

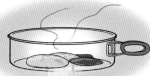

Method

1. Chop the garlic and mix in a bowl with some olive oil, balsamic vinegar, and seasoning.
2. Chop the red pepper into quarters and cover the pepper and mushrooms with the oil and vinegar mixture.
3. Heat some olive oil in a pan and cook the peppers, then the mushrooms, for three or four minutes on each side. Remove the skin from the pepper once cooked.
4. Fill each burger bun with a mushroom and red pepper quarter, then top with goat cheese and a generous handful of arugula. Eat right away.

BEAR SAYS

You can also make healthy burgers using grilled chicken breast or bean patties.

SIDE SALADS

Salad is very good for you, packed with vitamins and minerals. These side salads will go well with any of the main meals described so far, or they can be eaten on their own.

Green salad

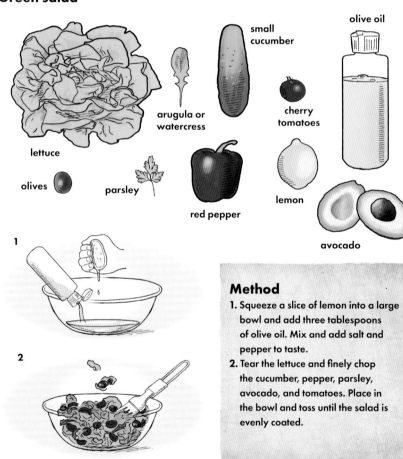

olive oil

small cucumber

cherry tomatoes

arugula or watercress

lettuce

olives

parsley

red pepper

lemon

avocado

1

2

Method
1. Squeeze a slice of lemon into a large bowl and add three tablespoons of olive oil. Mix and add salt and pepper to taste.
2. Tear the lettuce and finely chop the cucumber, pepper, parsley, avocado, and tomatoes. Place in the bowl and toss until the salad is evenly coated.

Chickpea and goat cheese salad

You need: canned chickpeas, 5 oz. goat cheese, cherry tomatoes, green pepper, ½ cucumber, parsley, olive oil, lemon, salt and pepper.

Method

1. Add three tablespoons of olive oil, a squeeze of lemon, salt, and pepper in a large bowl and mix together.
2. Drain the chickpeas. Cut the goat cheese into cubes and chop the cucumber, pepper, and tomatoes. Add these ingredients to the bowl and toss to coat with dressing.

BEAR SAYS

You may be able to forage arugula, watercress, and herbs from the wild. Arugula has a peppery taste that is great in salads.

Make a vinaigrette dressing

You need: olive oil, balsamic vinegar, Dijon mustard, lemon, seasoning

Method

1. Measure six tablespoons of olive oil and two tablespoons of balsamic vinegar into a jar. Add a generous squeeze of lemon, one teaspoon of Dijon mustard, and a pinch of salt and pepper. Put the lid on and shake to mix thoroughly, or stir with a spoon.

CAMPFIRE DESSERTS

Fruit desserts taste great outdoors! These recipes provide a treat around a campfire. A hot dessert can also boost morale if the weather turns cold or rainy.

Baked bananas

bananas

tinfoil

cinnamon

maple syrup or honey

Greek yogurt (optional)

lemon

BEAR SAYS

Foil packages baked in a fire contain hot juices! Be careful as you open them, and allow the contents to cool before tasting.

Method

1. Peel the bananas and place in thick foil. Add a squeeze of lemon juice and a pinch of cinnamon. Close the foil to make a tight package. Wearing gloves, place in the embers using tongs.

2. Cook for 15–20 minutes, then remove with tongs. Carefully open the package and serve with a drizzle of maple syrup or honey, and Greek yogurt if you like.

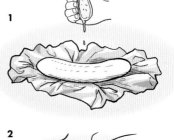

1

2

Fruit kebabs

honey

fruit, such as apples, pears, peaches, or apricots

long skewers

Method

1. Thread the whole, unpeeled fruit onto long skewers or peeled sticks. Wearing gloves, toast over an open fire or grill.
2. When the fruit skin starts to peel, remove from the heat and drizzle with honey. Return to the heat until the honey caramelizes. Then remove from the heat and allow to cool before eating.

1

2

Grilled fruit

Fruit such as plums, peaches, and apples can also be roasted on a barbecue grill. Cut the fruit into halves and place round-side up on the grill. Roast for three or four minutes, then turn over and sprinkle with cinnamon. Cook for another three or four minutes, then serve with maple syrup or honey and yogurt.

MORE DESSERTS

These two simple desserts will round off an evening by the campfire perfectly! You don't even need a fire or a stove to cook them, so they're perfect for beginners.

Campfire mess

packaged meringues

raspberries, strawberries, or blueberries

heavy cream

BEAR SAYS

This is a version of an English dessert called Eton mess. It was invented when an excited dog squashed a dessert being delivered to Eton College, an English boarding school.

1

2

Method
1. Chop the fruit. Break the meringues into a bowl. Whip the heavy cream, add to the ingredients, and stir.
2. Serve immediately.

Tutti-frutti salad

  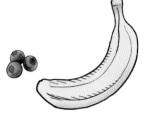

your favorite fruit—try apples, berries, bananas, grapes, pineapple, or peaches

Greek yogurt (optional)

1

2

Method

1. Peel the fruit if necessary. Cut into small chunks and place in a bowl. Add three tablespoons of orange juice and mix together.
2. Serve as is, or with Greek yogurt if you like.

CAMPFIRE TREATS

What better way to spend time around the campfire than swapping tales while toasting marshmallows? S'mores is a marshmallow recipe invented by the Girl Scouts on camping trips in the early 1920s.

Toasted marshmallows

marshmallows

metal or wooden skewers, or sticks

BEAR SAYS

You can peel green, sap-filled sticks to use as skewers. Or use packaged wooden skewers and soak them in water for at least half an hour before using.

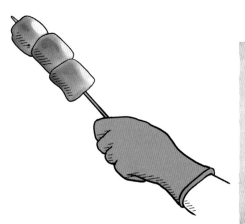

Method
Thread one to three marshmallows onto sticks or wooden skewers. Toast over a campfire or barbecue grill for a few minutes until golden on the outside. You can prop the skewers near the fire, or wear gloves to shield your hands from the heat.

S'mores

marshmallows

thin chocolate
divided into
squares

graham
crackers

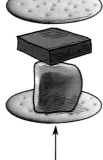

Method
Toast marshmallows over a campfire or barbecue grill until golden. Place a hot marshmallow on a graham cracker. Put a piece of chocolate on top. Cover with another graham cracker and squish down slightly. Serve warm. I once ate these with a president of the United States on a hiking expedition with him in Alaska! These were his favorite treat!

Fruity s'mores
Prepare in the same way as basic s'mores, but add a layer of sliced fruit sandwiched between the chocolate and the graham cracker.

marshmallows

thin chocolate
divided into squares

graham
crackers

your choice of fruit, such as berries or banana

Extra tip
Don't hold marshmallows too close to the fire or they will burn. The gooey insides are very hot, so allow them to cool before you eat them.

GLOSSARY

Caramelize – when sugar turns to a brown syrup when heated.

Carbohydrates – a group of nutrients found in foods such as fruit, vegetables, grains, beans, and dairy products. Carbohydrates provide us with most of our energy.

Ember – a glowing spark.

Firesteel – a device for lighting fires, made of a metal rod and a striker, which is scraped along the rod to produce a spark.

Forage – to look for food in the wild.

Friction – a force produced when one object rubs against another.

Fuzz stick – a stick that has been partially splintered. The splinters help the stick catch fire.

Green wood – freshly cut, sap-filled timber that does not burn well.

Guacamole – a dip made from avocados.

Ignite – to set fire to something.

Kindling – small fuel, such as thin sticks, used to feed a newly lit fire.

Morale – confidence or good spirits.

Protein – a nutrient found in foods such as meat, fish, milk, eggs, nuts, and beans, that allows cells and the body to grow.

Purify – to remove dangerous substances from water.

Spatula – a cooking tool with a wide, blunt blade.

Suspend – to hang something, usually in midair.

Tinder – very dry fuel used to catch a spark to light a fire.

Discover all the books in the
Bear Grylls Outdoor Skills Handbook series:

Kane Miller, A Division of EDC Publishing, 2024

Bonnier Books UK in partnership with Bear Grylls Ventures
Produced by Bonnier Books UK
Copyright © 2018 Bonnier Books UK

For information contact:

Kane Miller, A Division of EDC Publishing

5402 S 122nd E Ave

Tulsa, OK 74146

www.kanemiller.com | www.paperpie.com

Library of Congress Control Number: 2023944004

Printed in China

1 2 3 4 5 6 7 8 9 10

ISBN: 978-1-68464-919-8

Disclaimer
Bonnier Books UK, Bear Grylls, and Kane Miller take pride in doing their best to get the facts right in putting together the information in this book, but occasionally something slips past us. Therefore, we make no warranties about the accuracy or completeness of the information in the book and to the maximum extent permitted, we disclaim all liability. Wherever possible, we will endeavor to correct any errors of fact at reprint.

Kids—if you want to try any of the activities in this book, please ask your parents first! Parents—all outdoor activities carry some degree of risk and we recommend that anyone participating in these activities be aware of the risks involved and seek professional instruction and guidance. None of the health/medical information in this book is intended as a substitute for professional medical advice; always seek the advice of a qualified practitioner.